DIDDY SHUM SHUM STANDS TALL

Rich McWatt
Illustrated By Calvin Innes

R McWatt Publishing

R McWatt Publishing
43 Beverley Road . Dunswell . HU6 0AD

Copyright © 2015 Rich McWatt
All rights reserved

Illustrations & Cover by Calvin Innes.

First Print 2015
by R McWatt Publishing
Printed in the United Kingdom

ISBN-13: 978-0-9932248-3-6

This book is sold subject to the condition that it shall not, by way of trade or otherwise, be lent, re-sold, hired out, or otherwise circulated without the publisher's prior consent in any form or binding or cover other than that in which it is published and without a similar condition including this condition being imposed on the subsequent purchaser.

British library Cataloguing in Publication Data
A CIP catalogue record for this book is available from the British Library

www.theshumshums.co.uk

Dedicated To

Pat and Maria, without your support and help over the years we would never be where we are.

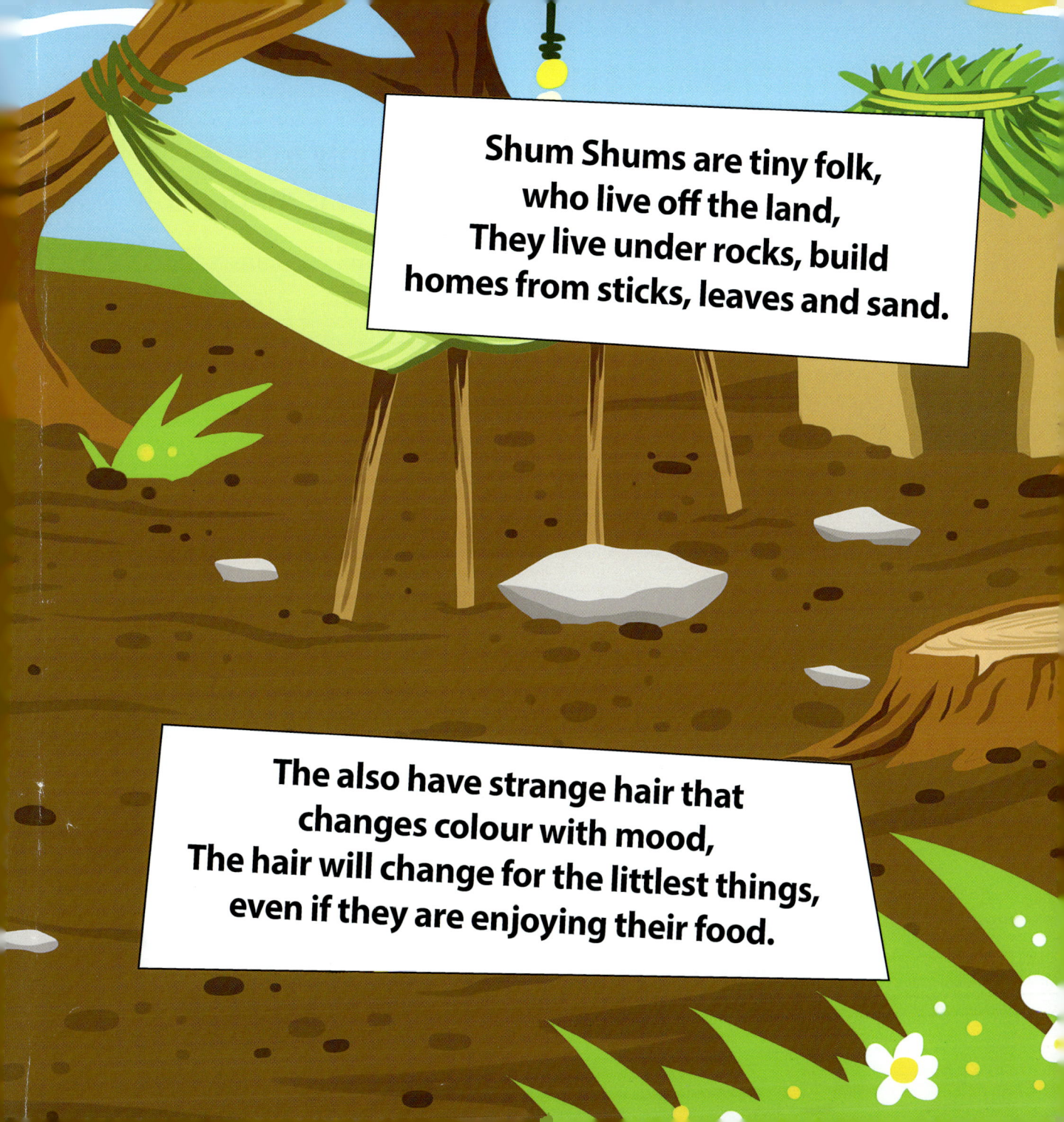

Shum Shums are tiny folk,
who live off the land,
They live under rocks, build
homes from sticks, leaves and sand.

The also have strange hair that
changes colour with mood,
The hair will change for the littlest things,
even if they are enjoying their food.

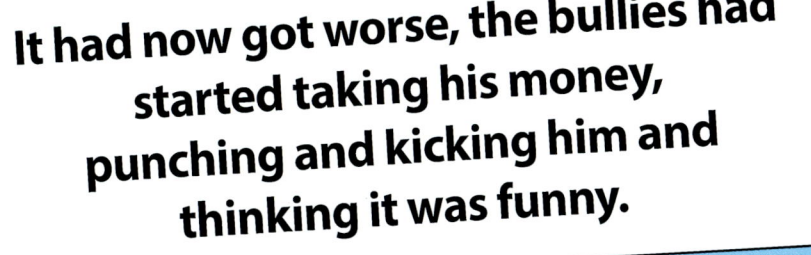

It had now got worse, the bullies had started taking his money, punching and kicking him and thinking it was funny.

Diddy rushed into school, keeping himself hidden well, he was so scared but didn't know who he could tell.

He couldn't tell his mother, Mama Kay Kay,
For he knew exactly what she would say.

She would say 'Diddy, you tell me who
they are and what they look like,
I'll get down there on my bike.'

'I'll give them a clip around the ear,
and that will stop them picking on you, my dear.'

Diddy was sure this is how she would react, and saw,
that her actions would end up breaking the law.

She was tough and strong was his mum,
and was once Shum Shum, sumo champion.

She had beaten Shum Shums from all over the land, and had stood there proud with the trophy in her hand.

So Diddy knew he couldn't tell Mama Kay Kay, for he was worried about the trouble that may come her way.

Kegger Greenwood was his teacher and he liked her a lot, although at times she spoke so much in class, the children thought she had lost the plot.

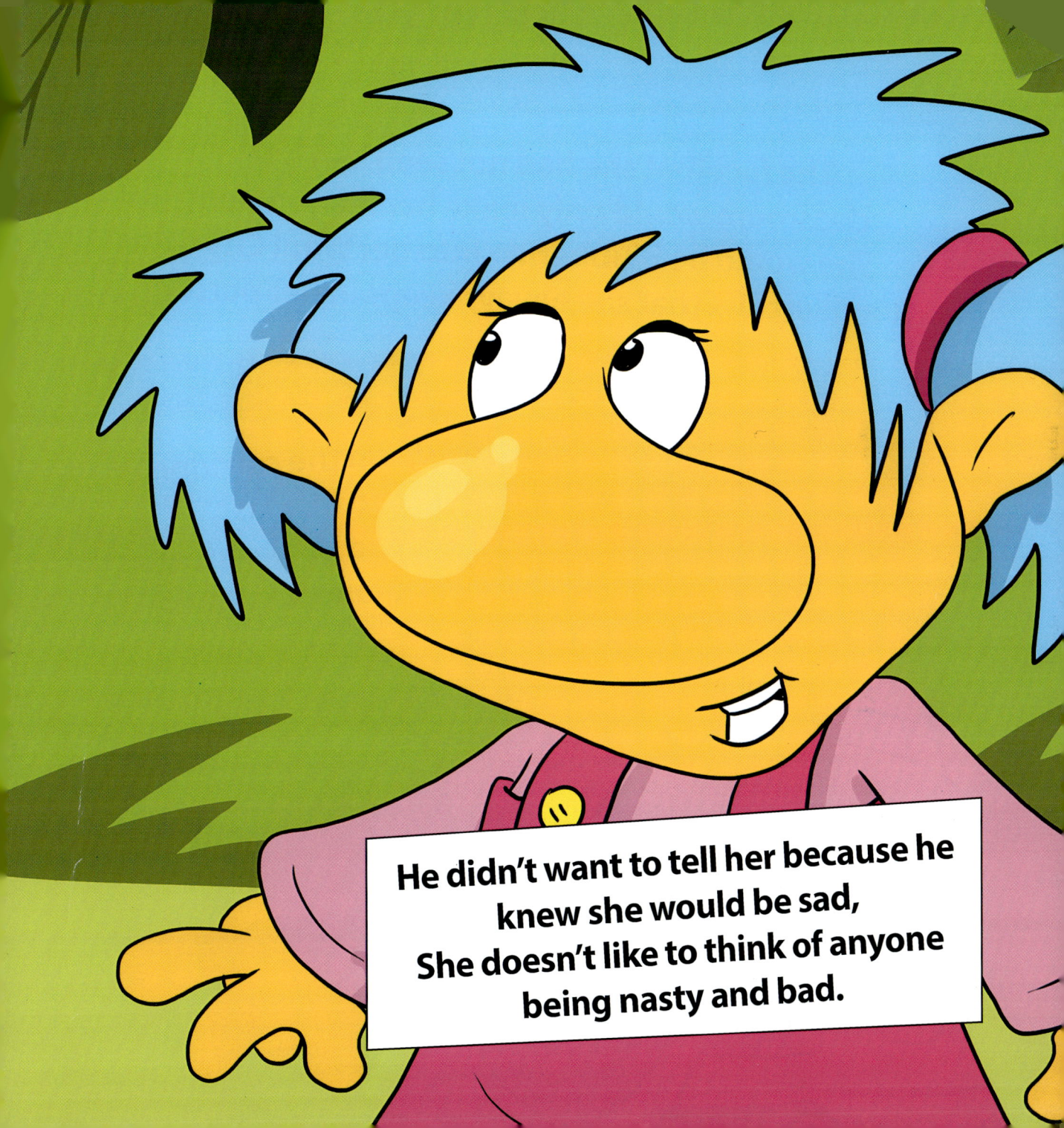

The fact that she had not seen it in her classroom would only make her feel worse. She would be blubbering into her Wool City handkerchief that she always keeps in her purse.

Rushing down the corridor, heading to his class, He had his head bowed down looking at no-one he passed.

He burst into tears and ran from the class.
He ran straight out of school, to the stream
and the long grass.

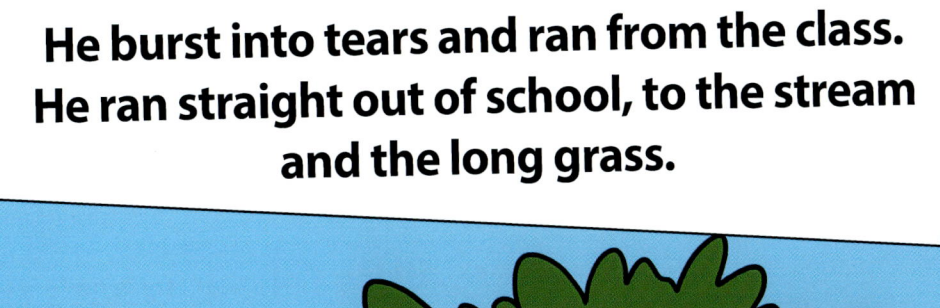

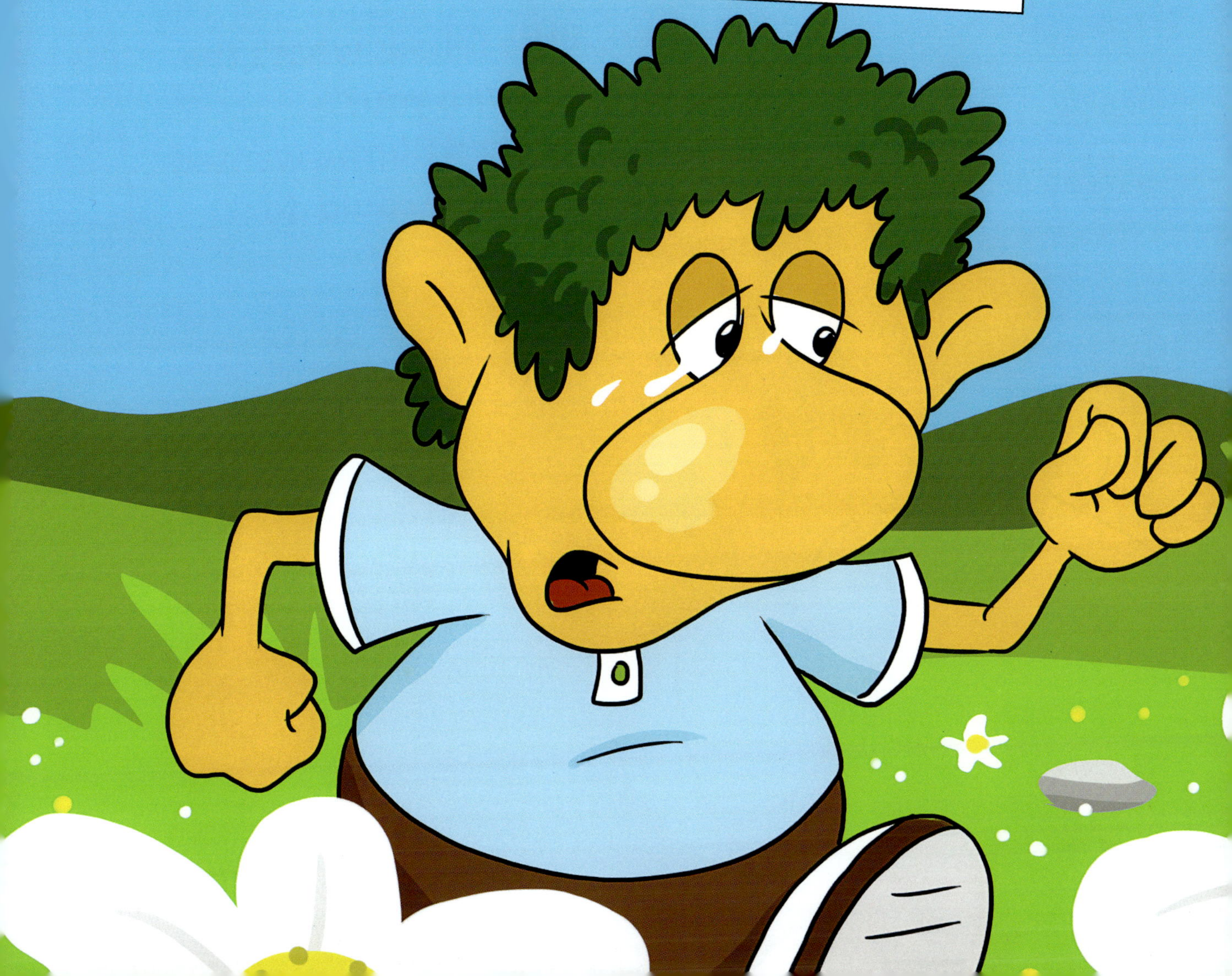

"Well, have you stood up to the boys
and told them to stop?"
"I wish I could but I'm small and they are not".

Blurbo pondered, wondering what he could do.
"I tell you what Diddy, I'll come to school with you".

Blurbo is well known as he is a great football player,
as was his father, Blooney Sayer.

"If I come to school and we speak to your head",
Diddy looked so scared, so full of dread.

There were whispers on the playground that Diddy was with a famous football player. Even the bullies were impressed, "He's friend's with Blurbo Sayer!'

Blurbo and Diddy spoke with Kegger, then the head, Diddy explained all that had happened and all that had been said.

Diddy met Dook and they talked through what had gone on.
Dook said he picked on him as he didn't look strong.

They talked for a while then
went out to play.
They played football with their
class, who all had plenty to say.

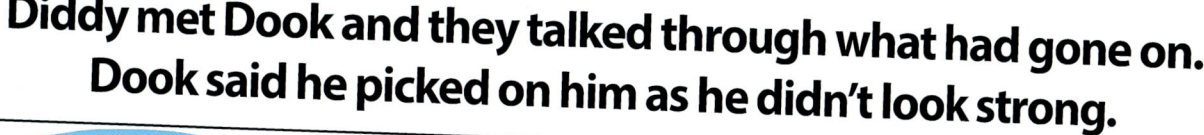

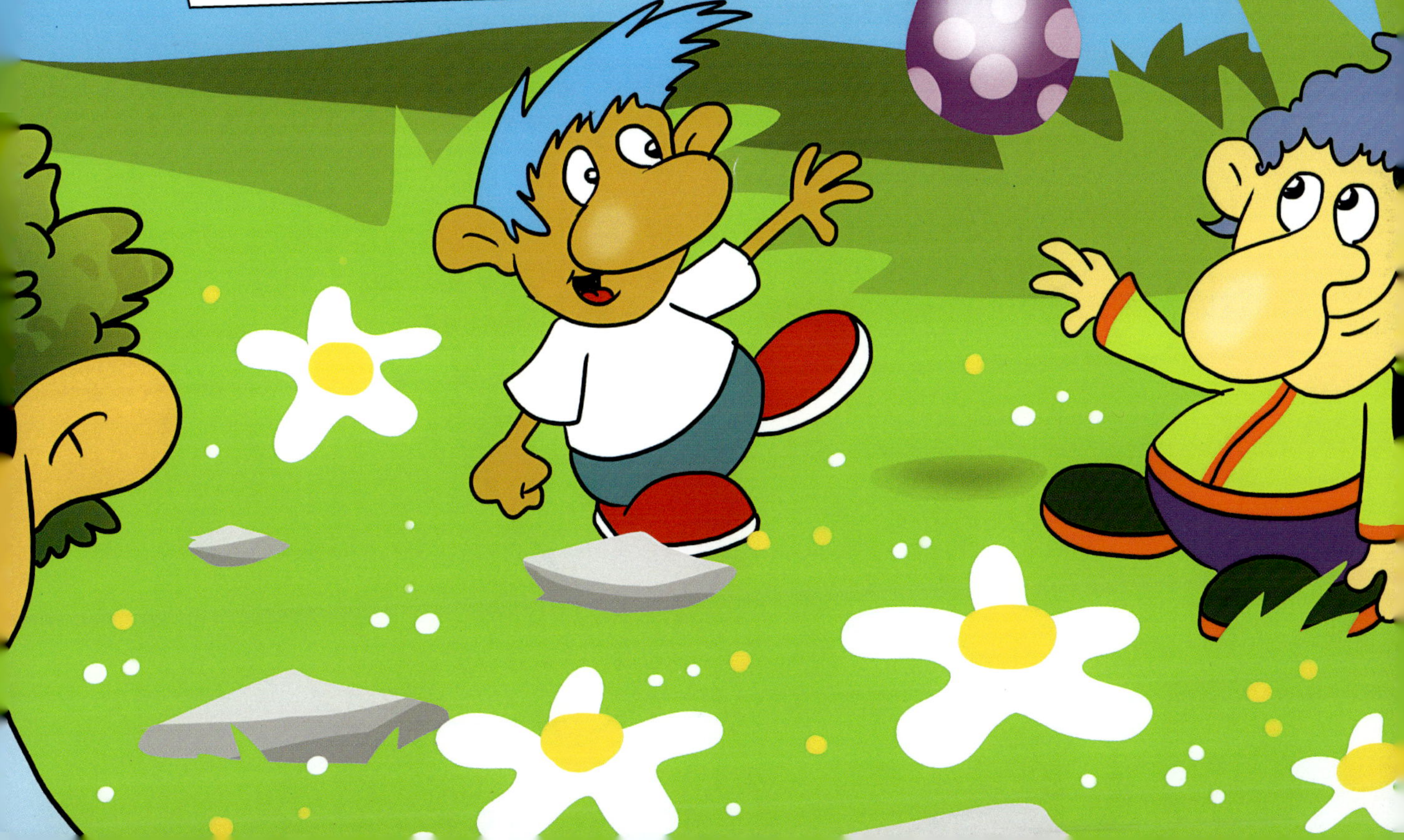

After Blurbo left Diddy he went to visit Evie Ann. Evie was his friend, the link between Shum Shum and human.

He told Evie about Diddy and what had been done. "Bullying is so bad, it doesn't need to go on".

"Well done for getting Diddy to talk it through, I am so very proud of you".

Blurbo blushed and his hair turned a dark red, "Evie you always embarrass me and make me look like a tomato head!"

"Don't be silly Blurbo, you are such a good Shum Shum,
I am so proud to have you as my best chum".

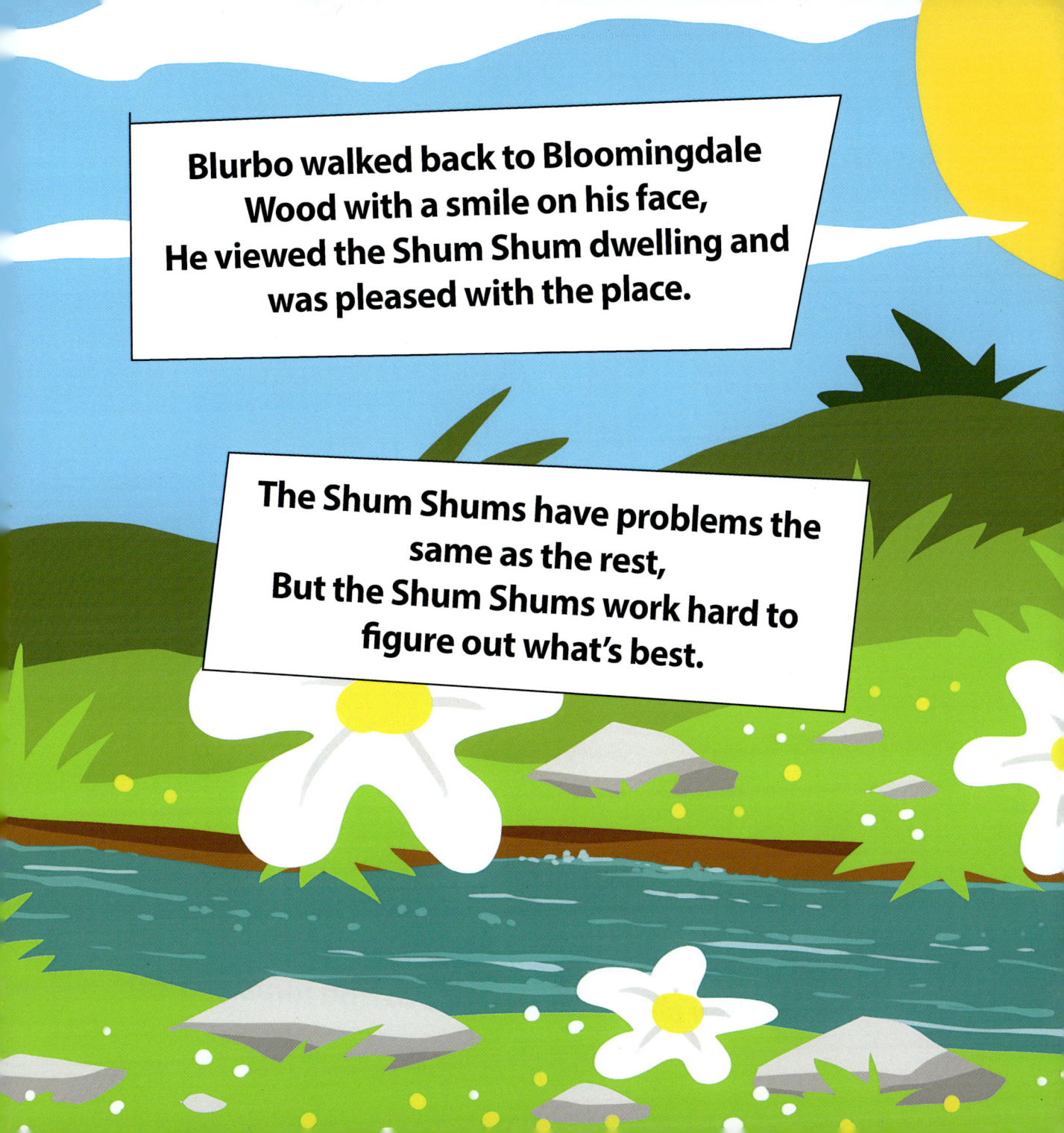

Blurbo walked back to Bloomingdale Wood with a smile on his face,
He viewed the Shum Shum dwelling and was pleased with the place.

The Shum Shums have problems the same as the rest,
But the Shum Shums work hard to figure out what's best.